D0811099

Pupil Parliament

by Sally Hewitt

Photographs by Chris Fairclough

© 2002 Franklin Watts

First published in 2002 by
Franklin Watts
96 Leonard Street
LONDON
EC2A 4XD

Franklin Watts Australia
56 O'Riordan Street
Alexandria
NSW 2015

ISBN: 0 7496 4367 6
Dewey Decimal Classification 324
A CIP catalogue reference for this book is available from the British
Library.

Printed in Malaysia

Editor: Kate Banham
Designer: Joelle Wheelwright
Art Direction: Peter Scoulding
Photography: Chris Fairclough

Acknowledgements
The publishers would like to thank the staff and pupils of Stanley
Junior School, Teddington, for their help in the production of this
book. The photograph on page 8 was supplied by Format
Photographers (© Jacky Chapman/Format). The photograph of York
House on page 20 was kindly supplied by Richmond upon Thames
borough council. The photographs on pages 21t, 25b and 26b were
supplied by the author.

Contents

(Words printed in **bold italics** are explained in the glossary.)

The Pupil Parliament

In the UK we live in a **democracy**, which means **government** by the people. Every four or five years we hold a **General Election** to choose who we want to represent us in **Parliament**.

On election day, everyone *votes*. ↗

The Pupil Parliament

Every year, all the schools in Richmond upon Thames learn about democracy by holding their own elections. Each school elects a boy and a girl to represent them at the Pupil Parliament. All the pupils in year 5 can take part. They might decide to stand for election themselves, or they might help with someone else's **campaign**.

The Pupil Parliament is good because it helps you to make the right decisions when you're older about who is the best person to vote for – not just who your friend is, but who you think would be best at it.

Questions

Is democracy a good way of running a country?

Do you think a Pupil Parliament is a good way of teaching children about democracy?

MPPs

The Members of the Pupil Parliament, the MPPs, are elected for a year. They meet three times during that year. Their first meeting is Pupil Parliament Day when they choose a topic to work on during the two follow-up Action Days.

↑ **The members of the Pupil Parliament enjoy working together on the Action Days.**

Pupil Parliament Meetings

PUPIL PARLIAMENT DAY
Choosing a topic.

ACTION DAY 1
Workshops to follow up topic.

ACTION DAY 2
More workshops to produce material for use back in school.

on the web

One year, the Pupil Parliament's topic was 'Refugees'. The MPPs met some refugee children and learned what life was like for them. The work they did was featured on the website of *Global Eye* magazine. Other schools could log on and find out about the Pupil Parliament and their work. Check it out at www.globaleye.org.uk/primary/action.

Your Local MP

 The Pupil Parliament helps children learn about how our country is governed, how people are elected to Parliament and what happens there.

Candidates

To become a **Member of Parliament** (MP) you must first become a **candidate** and stand for election. The candidate with the most votes becomes a Member of Parliament. Their job as an MP is to represent everyone in their **constituency** (area), even those who didn't vote for them, until the next General Election comes around.

↑ **Shortly before a General Election, candidates try to persuade people to vote for them.**

Political parties

Most MPs are members of one of the big political parties – Labour, Conservative or Liberal Democrat.

8

Jenny Tonge

One of the Pupil Parliament's local MPs is Jenny Tonge who is a Liberal Democrat. She likes to work with schools in the borough, so when she was invited to visit the Pupil Parliament, she said 'yes'.

Jenny Tonge likes to work with pupils of all ages. →

Jenny Tonge enjoyed seeing the Pupil Parliament in action.

> *We had a very good day. I went along and listened to the pupils actually talking about issues that concerned them. It was very good to see the children able to stand up and make speeches.*

> *One of the lovely things about the House of Commons is that people don't just make speeches. We are always arguing with one other, so a speech becomes a little debate.*

Debates

She believes that debates are an important part of democracy and that everyone should have the chance to express their opinions.

For the Pupil Parliament, all year 5 pupils in Richmond schools have the chance to become a candidate. Their school is their constituency, and the voters are the other pupils.

↑ Alex (right) and Harry (left) talk to their friends about becoming a candidate.

Harry and Alex

Harry and Alex both stood as candidates for Stanley Junior School. Deciding to take part means taking on a lot of hard work so all the candidates must be sure they really want to do it.

> I'd thought about it since I came into the school in year 3. I always said I really wanted to do it, so when it came around in year 5, I went for it.

Campaign

Every candidate runs a campaign to persuade the voters that they are the best person to vote for. First, they have to choose a campaign manager and team. Next, they have to decide what subject to campaign on. Then the speech has to be researched and written and the campaign planned – and they only have four weeks to do it all!

↑ **'Do you like my poster?'**

Harry's campaign manager gave him lots of support and encouragement. ↑

Campaign managers

The campaign manager's job is to help the candidate with their speech, manage the money, organise making posters and stickers, and make sure everyone knows who their candidate is and what they stand for.

I wanted to drop out, but my campaign manager said, 'Come on, we've got this far and we want to get a bit further!'

Question

Why do you think the campaign manager's job is important?

The campaigns

 The candidates had to campaign for things that could really happen. It was no good thinking of a scheme that would be far too expensive or impossible to carry out.

Helpful hints

Their teachers offered some helpful hints to the campaign teams.

- Make posters to attract voters.
- Put them where everyone can see them.
- Make badges and stickers.
- Write leaflets.

Hot topics

Twelve candidates stood for election at Stanley Junior School. Here are some of the topics and slogans they chose.

MODERN LEISURE FACILITIES

Put your X by my name if you want to play the game.

AGAINST BULLYING

Let's work together to keep this a bully-free school and a great place to be.

REDUCE POLLUTION

Remember – our environment now, our children's future.

ADVENTURE PLAYGROUNDS

If you want more fun outdoors, vote for Harry and adventure playgrounds.

Possible issues

Pollution and saving endangered species are big issues that affect the whole world, but there are always things that everyone can do to help. A bully-free school or an adventure playground are things that affect the local community.

Keeping accounts

To make it fair, each team was only allowed to spend £5, and had to account for what they spent.

Sophia's team made stickers to give to their supporters.

'Always wear your sticker!'

'Everyone will see our poster here.'

I got information about pollution and the environment off the internet and I phoned people.

Question

Why would it be unfair if some teams had more money to spend than others?

The Speeches

Every candidate had to deliver a speech to the school during assembly. They only had two minutes to get everyone's attention and put over their point. Boring the audience would be a big mistake!

The candidates and campaign managers checked the speeches together.

Speech

Hi! I am Sophia Zhang, and this is my campaign manager Gemma Hornsey. I am a candidate for Pupil Parliament. I think that being a good citizen means that you do not only think of yourself, but that you think of all the other people in your community too. You would make decisions to suit everybody in your group so nobody is left out. You would respect everybody in your group. You would think of the environment around you and ways of making it better. Pollution is one of the reasons why our environment is not as good as it could be.

Our main aim is to try and help reduce the current amount of pollution there is. There are many forms of pollution: smoking, car fumes, litter, and many more. There are many ways in our everyday lives that we make pollution, but there are also many ways in our everyday lives that we could reduce pollution. Things such as throwing litter on the floor can be easily helped: you would just throw your own litter in the bin - simple.

Recycling is another way of helping the environment, reusing materials to make new products so that these materials are not wasted.

To help recycle more, I would like to suggest that there could be recycling points for cans and bottles for the school, like there are for newspapers, but outside the main gates. So that it is convenient for parents to recycle the cans they have used at home, as they collect their children.

Your vote will help us work to reduce the current amount of pollution in the environment, in an area near you. It will give us cleaner air, and it will help your health. It will also help your future generations of children so that they do not get worse if they have illnesses such as asthma, because of all the pollution.

Thank you for listening. Remember, our environm...
...ure.

Helpful hints

The teachers had more advice for the candidates.

• Time your speech – it should only last 2 minutes.

• Practise delivering your speech.

• Your speech should be interesting. Will people want to listen to it?

• Tape your speech and listen to yourself.

Anti-litter

The children listened to an anti-litter speech. They heard how they can all help to fight pollution by throwing their rubbish away and keeping their own environment clean and tidy.

Actions and props made the speech more dramatic. ↓

↑ **Questions were taken from the floor.**

Questions

What issue would you campaign on?

What title would you give your speech?

Harry says:

My campaign was to get more adventure playgrounds in the area. Neighbouring boroughs have got really good adventure playgrounds and we haven't really got any.

Alex says:

My campaign was about endangered animals and what we could do to help a whole endangered species.

Election Day

 After four weeks of campaigning, it was time for the voters to make up their minds. All the schools taking part held their election on the same Thursday. Children from year 6 were in charge. They still had a vote, even though they would be leaving at the end of term.

Voting slip

BOYS		GIRLS	
Harry Ford (Adventure playgrounds)	X	Alex Hook (Endangered species)	
Adam Barker (Leisure facilities)		Chloë Wood (Bullying)	
Stevie Lewis (Pollution)		Nancy Holdenby (Pollution)	
Tom Webb (Anti-smoking)		Amy Joseph (Pollution)	
Bernard Redman (Leisure centres)		Sophia Zhang (Pollution)	X
		Poppy Croft (Pollution)	
		Jennifer Savage (Graffiti)	

↑ The voting slips showed the name of each candidate and what they were standing for.

Secret ballot

In the general election, voters can keep their vote a secret. This is called a secret ballot. The ballot for the Pupil Parliament was secret too.

> The secret ballot gave me confidence to vote for who I really think is best and not just who my friends think I should vote for.

Voting

Each voter was given their own number. As they came into the gym to vote, their number was

checked off on a list and they were given a voting slip. They took this into a booth and put a cross next to the names of one girl and one boy. Then they folded the voting slip and put it in the ballot box.

Everyone voted one by one. →

All the votes were counted.

counting the votes

When all the votes had been cast, the doors to the gym were shut and no one was allowed in. Then every vote was counted by the counting clerks. Their job was to mark each vote on to a tally sheet and do the final count.

Tally sheet

BOYS

Harry	Adam	Stevie	Tom	Bernard		
Ⲗⲏⲧ	//	////	///	//		

GIRLS

Alex	Chloe	Nancy	Amy	Sophia	Poppy	Jennifer
Ⲗⲏⲧ	/	//	//	///	//	/

The Winners

Later on the same day, when all the votes had been counted, everyone gathered in the gym to see who had won.

Announcing the winners

The candidates stood at the front with the returning officer whose job it was to announce the winners. They didn't know the results. The returning officer waited until everyone was quiet, unfolded his piece of paper and said, 'The winners are... Alex and Harry!'

↑ When the winners were announced the whole school clapped and cheered.

congratulations

Then the winners and their campaign managers congratulated each other. It was important for Alex and Harry to get on well. They were going to be doing a lot of work together.

'Well done!' ↗

After the excitement of winning had died down, the children who voted for them talked about why they thought Alex and Harry had won.

I really like animals, and Alex was talking about animals in the rainforest, and how the trees shouldn't be cut down because there wouldn't be any wildlife and nature.

I'm glad Harry won the Pupil Parliament place, because he wrote a very good speech and he made good points.

I voted for the people who didn't get shy and had great ideas.

Pupil Parliament Day

 The first big event for the new Members of the Pupil Parliament was at York House in Twickenham. They met in the council chambers and sat on the councillors' big green chairs.

The MPPs met in the council chambers at York House.

Harry and Alex had to give their speeches again.

It was really hard cutting my speech down to just one minute.

It was really nerve-racking because there were all these people just watching you at the podium.

Speeches

The first business of the day was to hear all 60 MPPs deliver their speeches. It took a long time, even though everyone had cut their speeches down to less than a minute. The MPPs graded each others' speeches to help them decide who to vote for to be *mayor* (leader) of the Pupil Parliament.

The new mayor

Caitlin was elected to be the Pupil Parliament's mayor for the year. Her speech was about traffic safety, helping the environment and the difference children can make even though they are only young.

I love being mayor. I have to make speeches and I have to welcome people and say goodbye. And sometimes I have to do a bit of work arranging what we do.

↑ **Everyone was impressed with Caitlin's speech.**

The new resolution

The MPPs then had to decide on a resolution. This is a statement that explains the theme for the work they would do during their year in office.

This is the resolution the MPPs chose.

We, the Pupil Parliament, will aim to raise awareness of the effects of drug abuse and will encourage children to participate in a healthy lifestyle.

On Action Day 1, all the MPPs got together to work on their resolution – to promote healthy living and drugs awareness. Caitlin, the Pupil Parliament mayor, gave the welcoming speech and then the day began.

Healthy Choices

To introduce the topic, Gill, a health education co-ordinator, talked about growing up and about making healthy or unhealthy choices. To make healthy choices you need to have good information and think about what is right for you.

Graham talked about drugs awareness.

Gill got everyone thinking.

Drugs

The MPPs then split into groups to hear the three speakers. Graham is a youth worker. He told them that drugs are substances people take that change the way they feel and think. The MPPs wanted to know what drugs do to you and why people take them.

Keeping fit

Alun, a youth development officer for rugby, talked about playing rugby and why children should play sport. He answered questions on how much exercise you should take and which sports are good for fitness.

↑ Alun's talk was about sport and exercise.

Gill's talk was on relationships. ↑

friends and family

Gill spoke again, this time about relationships. The MPPs decided that the most important people in their lives were their mum and dad and then their friends. They were surprised to find out that in three or four years' time they would probably think their friends were more important than their parents.

Good Question!

After listening to the talks, the MPPs wanted to find out what the children in their schools really knew about diet, drugs, growing up and relationships.

They thought about what questions to ask. ↑

Back at school, each child ↑ filled in a questionnaire.

Questionnaire

They decided to produce a questionnaire. This is a list of questions designed to find out what people know, what they don't know, and what they think about a particular subject. The questions needed a simple 'yes' or 'no' answer, e.g.

• Is your diet healthy?

• Are all drugs dangerous?

• Are you nervous about moving to secondary school?

Action Day 2

At Action Day 2, the MPPs discussed the answers to the questionnaires. The results from one school showed that nearly everyone did some kind of exercise every day. Only about half of the children thought they had a healthy diet. They all thought they should be taught about drugs. Most children were worried about growing up.

The health questionnaire results showed how much the pupils knew. ↗

The Pupil Parliament Questionnaire ⊠
How health conscious are you?

Diet

Are you a boy or a girl?	Boy	49%	Girl	51%
Are you happy about your weight?	Yes	85%	No	15%
Do you do some sort of exercise every day?	Yes	98%	No	22
Is your diet healthy?	Yes	49%	No	51%
Do you eat more fruit than snacks?	Yes	0%	No	100%
Are you a fit person?	Yes	0%	No	100%

Drugs

Are all drugs dangerous?	Yes	15%	No	85%
Do you think cigarettes and alcohol are proper drugs?	Yes	85%	No	15
Can you name 5 illegal drugs?	Yes	13%	No	87%
Should children be taught about drugs?	Yes	100%	No	0%

Growing up and relationships

Are you nervous about moving to secondary school?	Yes	47%	No	53%
At the moment, who are the most important to you: friends or family?	Friends	99%	Family	1%
Are you worried about growing up?	Yes	91%	No	9%
What is more important to you: looks or personality?	Looks	0%	Personality	100%

Poster power

The MPPs then set to work producing posters for National Health Week. They chose topics based on the answers to the questionnaire. Using bright coloured pastels, felt-tip pens, coloured paper and pictures cut out of magazines, they designed eye-catching posters with slogans to make you stop and think.

Question

Why is a questionnaire a good way of finding out what people know and think?

At the end of the day, the posters were taken back to put up in their schools. ↑

It's the end of another good year for the Pupil Parliament. It would soon be time for this year's MPPs to help organise the next Pupil Parliament election.

It gives children a chance to state their own opinions on things.

The MPPs have enjoyed their year in office.

Democracy is fun

The children agree that it's fun to learn about democracy by holding an election. They have learned how important it is to be able to put over their own point of view and to be able to vote for the candidate of their choice.

 The MPPs have their last lunch together.

Standing for election

Holding elections every year means that all the children get a chance to vote and to be candidates when their turn comes around. Now Alex and Harry are in year 6, and it's nearly time to choose the next two MPPs. Children in year 5 now have to decide whether they want to stand for election. They have been voting for two years now, so they have had plenty of time to see what it's like. When they discussed it together, some felt confident that they could be a candidate but others weren't so sure.

I do a lot of stage acting... I wouldn't be shy in front of everybody.

You have to put a lot of work into it. It's not just something you can do in a day.

They must have taken a long time preparing for it. I'm not exactly sure that I'd be able to do a speech that long.

I want to be a candidate because I want to make everything better for everyone.

Glossary

Campaign A campaign is a plan of action to get something done (to achieve a goal). Giving speeches, making posters and talking to voters are all part of an election campaign.

Candidate A candidate is someone who applies for a job or stands for election.

Constituency The whole country is divided into areas called constituencies. People who live in each constituency elect a Member of Parliament to represent them.

Democracy Democracy means government by the people. Britain is a democracy because the people choose their government by holding elections.

General Election To elect means to make a choice. In a General Election, voters all over the country choose their Member of Parliament.

Government The government manages the country. The political party, such as Labour, Conservative or Liberal Democrat, that wins the most votes in the General Election forms the government.

Mayor The mayor is the head of the local council which runs local government. He or she wears a chain of office and holds the post for one year.

Member of Parliament A Member of Parliament is the candidate who received the most votes in their constituency in the General Election. Their job in Parliament is to represent everyone in their constituency.

Parliament The British Parliament is made up of the Queen, the House of Lords and the House of Commons. Parliament is where new laws are debated and voted for.

Vote When you vote, you make one choice from several choices. To vote in a General Election you put a cross by the candidate you would like to be your Member of Parliament.

Taking Part

Meet your local MP

Richmond MPs support the Pupil Parliament, visit schools and sometimes take groups of children to the House of Commons.

Invite your local MP to visit your school and talk about his or her work. You may get an invitation to visit the House of Commons.

Visit your local council chambers

The Pupil Parliament meets once a year in the local council chambers where they meet the mayor and some of the councillors.

Arrange a visit to your local council chambers. It's a good way to learn about the work of your local government.

Hold an election

The Pupil Parliament holds an election once a year. Some schools hold their own election during a general election.

Learn about democracy by holding an election. Try to make sure the elected candidates have a chance of making real changes in your school or in your local community.

Work with other schools

Members of the Pupil Parliament get a chance to meet and work with pupils from other local schools.

Find out if schools in your area would like to set up a Pupil Parliament. If so, ask your MP and local councillors to support you.

Index